Santa Claus

Saint, Shaman, and Symbol

Santa Claus

Saint, Shaman, and Symbol

Bill Palmer

Anamchara Books

Copyright © 2014 by Anamchara Books, a division of Harding House Publishing Service, Inc. All rights reserved. No part of this publication may be reproduced or transmitted in any form or by any means, electronic or mechanical, including photocopying, recording, taping, or any information storage and retrieval system, without permission from the publisher.

Anamchara Books
Vestal, New York 13850

9 8 7 6 5 4 3 2 1

IngramSpark 2020 paperback ISBN: 978-1-62524-790-2

Author: Bill Palmer

Book design and production by Vestal Creative Services. www.vestalcreative.com.

*In loving memory of my parents:
Brian Charles Palmer, Jr.,
and Mary Claire Snedecor Palmer
and to the eternal honor
of Saint Nicholas of Myra*

Contents

Introduction	9
1. The Pagan Origins of Christmas: The Shamanic Santa Claus	15
2. The Real Saint Nick	27
3. Saint Nicholas Comes to Europe	35
4. *Sinterklaas Komt!* (Saint Nicholas Is Coming!)	43
5. Santa Claus Comes to America	51
6. Here Comes Santa Claus!	61
7. A "Saint" for the Twentieth Century	69
8. Keep the "Santa" in Santa Claus!	79

Introduction

He mounts to the chimney-top like a bird,
And drops to the hearth like stone.
The little red stockings he silently fills,
Till the stockings will hold no more;
The bright little sleds for the great snow hills
Are quickly set down on the floor.
Then Santa Claus mounts to the roof like a bird,
And glides to his seat in the sleigh;
Not the sound of a bugle or drum is heard
As he noiselessly gallops away.
Anonymous, 1880

Do you believe in Santa?

He may be the most well-known being—real or fictitious—on planet Earth. Think about that for a moment: Can you think of a single person you know who wouldn't immediately recognize the jolly fat man in the red suit? Can you even remember a time before you knew who Santa Claus was?

Among the vast pantheon of humankind's deities, ancient and modern—gods, goddesses, angels, demons, dictators, statesmen, movie stars, historical figures, sports heroes, billionaires, and prophets—Santa holds his own, and he has done so for over a thousand years. Santa Claus looms large in the consciousness of many hundreds of millions of people, from the squalling baby having her first picture taken with him at his headquarters at the mall to the grandfather reading "'Twas the Night Before Christmas" through sentiment-misted eyes. Throughout the Western world, in such various guises as Sinterklaas, Father Christmas, and Grandfather Frost, Santa presides over a year-end holiday season that brings families together, generates billions of dollars in sales, and combines deep nostalgia for a mythical past with hopes for a better year to come. In millions of homes where the birth of the Messiah barely registers as a cultural memory at Christmas, Santa is still very much a part of the season. And well beyond those parts of the world where Christmas is celebrated, Santa Claus is still one of the best-known icons of American culture.

Here we have a mythical being with origins in our most remote past (I'm going to suggest that Santa has links that go all the way back to the Ice Age), who yet remains not only famous and popular but still immensely vivid today in the twenty-first century. For literally a hundred or more generations, people have been sharing the tales and celebrating the power of Santa Claus and his kind. The delight of children, advertising icon, early American folk figure, Christian saint, midwinter deity—Santa Claus is all these things. He brings together, in one of the most beloved and familiar characters in our shared mythology, themes that are deeply spiritual. Santa's very identity is close to the heart of what it means to be a human being.

I can't help but think something very important is going on with Santa Claus. There has got to be a reason why we have carried him with us for so long, and continue to enthusiastically pass his legend along to the next generation. Santa Claus is important.

In these next chapters I'll share with you what I've learned about Santa Claus. I want to explore with you themes that range from cold-climate Earth Magic to the early Christian Church, from the medieval Cult of the Saints to the rise, triumph, and beginning-of-the-end of capitalism. Santa was there with us the whole time—shaman, saint, and symbol—with some true and abiding lessons to teach us all.

So, with a wind-blown flurry of snow and a jolly "ho, ho, ho" somewhere off in the distance, let's begin!

1
The Pagan Origins of Christmas: The Shamanic Santa Claus

In the bleak midwinter, frosty wind made moan,
earth stood hard as iron, water like a stone;
snow had fallen, snow on snow, snow on snow,
in the bleak midwinter, long ago.
Christina Rossetti

Who isn't dreaming of a white Christmas? I live in upstate New York, a place where Christmastime is almost always cold and often snowy, but from Pole to Pole, wherever Christmas is celebrated and whatever the climatalogical norm, the iconography of Christmas is most decidedly wintry. Everywhere, far beyond the natural range of the spruce and the fir, the festivities of the season take place around an evergreen tree (albeit one sometimes made of plastic). Under the tree, toy trains run through miniature towns covered with snow. Even the iconic nativity—a model of the stable in Bethlehem where the baby Jesus was born, set up at this time of year in many Christian homes—is often a snow scene. In my family's home the crèche was always a scene created with cotton batting and glitter—"in the bleak midwinter," as the old hymn tells us.

And here comes Santa Claus, right out of the North Pole—the place that is rumored to be the meteorological origin of all this Christmas-time snow and cold—dressed in a red, fur-trimmed parka and driving a sleigh pulled by magic reindeer, an ungulate species of the subarctic. After, perhaps magically, forcing his bulk down a chimney, he enters homes via a fireplace, which, he can only hope, is not banked with a fire against a cold Christmas Eve. His face is ruddy with cold, his "nose like a cherry," as he fills the stockings. Closer to or south of the Equator, Santa might arrive on a surfboard wearing a Hawaiian shirt, but it's always with a jokey wink. Santa is all about winter.

The Winter Solstice and the Birth of Christ

The date of Christmas coincides almost exactly with the Winter Solstice. In the Northern Hemisphere, this is the shortest day and the longest night of the year. It is the nadir of the natural year. From the beginning, Christmas has combined the Christian Church's commemoration of the birth of Jesus Christ with pre- and non-Christian customs and rituals associated with celebrations at the Winter Solstice. The age-old interplay between Christian joy at the promise of redemption through the Incarnation and pagan-influenced celebrations of light and life, feasting, and revelry continues to give Christmas its particular power.

But the interplay has also always held tension. Churchmen have been officially condemning the sensual excesses of Christmas celebrations for centuries. Every December, for more than a thousand years, official edicts were published, and priests railed from pulpits across Europe against the excessive consumption of food and alcohol; the hanging of evergreens; and dancing, singing, and dressing up in celebration of the Winter Solstice at the expense of a more "spiritual observation" of the Nativity of Jesus Christ. In the seventeenth century, English Puritans went so far as to legislate, by Act of Parliament, the abolition of any celebration of Christmas—religious or secular—declaring it both unscriptural and essentially sinful. Today, four hundred years later, preachers and editorial writers continue to bemoan the commercialization and materialism of the modern Christmas. Some Christians claim that secular society is engaged in an intentional cultural war against the religious observance of Jesus' birthday. For them, even the culturally neutral December wish of "Happy Holidays" is an insult to the Babe of Bethlehem and to the historical religious heritage of the majority of Americans. It is an old, old conflict.

In fact, the "secular" aspects of our modern Christmas—the feasting, the evergreens, the exchanging of gifts, the celebration of snow and cold weather—long predate its commemoration of the birth of Christ. The Christian gospels give us no reason at all to associate the birthday of a historical Jesus with the Winter Solstice. They actually hint at an early-spring date, since the shepherds, to whom the angels first announced the Good News, are said to have been "abiding in the fields, keeping watch over their flocks by night," which shepherds did at the time of year when lambs were born and most vulnerable to the elements and to predators—in February and March.

It is a very long story, but over the centuries the Christian Church made a series of decisions, conscious and otherwise, to associate its joyful celebration of the Nativity with ancient and well-established festivals celebrating the lengthening of the day and the victory of light over darkness (the "Sol Invictus," the "Unconquerable Sun" of the Roman mystery cults; the festivities of the Empire's New Year, the "Saturnalia"; and the even older northern European Yuletide).

Northern Earth Magic

Picture a late-December night long, long ago in Europe's Far North...

The cold is intense and the snow falls thickly around the little settlement of huts at the edge of the fir forest. The Old Man by the fire sips his brew of holy herbs. Muttering softly to himself, he spends the longest night of the year in and out of trance while the people sleep. Finally, in the weak, grey light of morning, he emerges from his hut. The people of his little community see him there, and they trudge through the deep snow to gather around him in great anticipation and not a little dread. They know the Old Man has been with the spirits. He tells the people how during the night he rose like vapor through the smoke hole of his hut. He flew through the snowy night in company with the ancestors, with the great hunters, and the legendary grandmothers of the people. They chased the spirits of the herd—the reindeer they depend upon for life itself—across the starry night sky. He traveled to the highest realms of the great and powerful gods, where there was feasting and singing. And now, his face ruddy with excitement, his eyes twinkling, he has a great gift for the people, a happy message from the spirit world: the winter will be long and hard, as it always is, but the days will lengthen, the cold will ease, and there will be many reindeer calves and fat new babies in the coming year. In the midst of these cold, dark, and sickly days, he has brought back luck to the hunt and health to the people. He chuckles with happiness, and the bells sewn on to his fur parka jingle in the frigid morning air.

As long ago and faraway as this story is, we can't help but recognize something familiar in it. Many of the essential elements of our modern Santa Claus go back to the very beginnings of anything we might call "Christmas." Semi-mythical beings, robust in build, dressed in furs, and personifying "Old Man Winter," are known all around the colder parts of the northern world. At their roots is one of the oldest and most sacred of humankind's spiritual heritage—the shamanic tradition.

Our ancestors, in every time and place, were deeply attuned to the natural world around them—to the life cycle of the plants and animals they depended upon for food, to the rhythm of the seasons, to the mysteries of birth and death and rebirth. At the same time, certain individuals within a community were often identified, for a variety of reasons, as having a particularly strong connection with the Otherworld. For untold thousands of years, shamans—holy men and women, priests and priestesses—led their communities in seasonal observances and rituals that helped to give meaning and structure to the community's experiences of the natural world. The shamans linked the ever-renewing round of time and weather, summer and winter to a deeper reality. They built a bridge between the world of everyday experience and the magical world. They traveled to the Spirit World, where they communed with the gods, with the ancestors, with the animal spirits. They returned to their communities to share with them the wisdom of the Spirits.

This shamanic tradition, this ancient earth magic, is unquestionably the oldest religious tradition of the human race. And our twenty-first century Santa Claus is genuinely a part of this ancient heritage.

Some of the very first "documents" of human spiritual life are the cave paintings of Ice Age southwestern Europe. Beginning 30,000 or so years ago in the dark recesses of caves during some of the coldest and most rigorous conditions our kind have ever faced, human beings painted images of the animals—reindeer and the now-extinct wooly rhinos and cold-adapted elephants—that they depended upon for their survival. Human figures, somewhat rare, are sometimes portrayed wearing the skins and antlers of these animals, suggesting a ritual union of human and animal spirits bringing luck to the hunt and meaning to the life of the tribe. These images may be the earliest depictions of shamans and shamanic rites.

The alternating bitter cold and milder cycles of the Pleistocene Epoch, from about 100,000 to 15,000 years ago, were formative years for the human species. Massive fields of glacial ice expanded and retreated over the centuries. In Europe, at the tundra-edge of the ice, small communities of hunters followed the herds of animals that were their livelihood for generations. Around the campfires at the mouths of caves and in the mammoth-bone and hide tents on the freezing, open plains, shamans communicated with the Spirits and told their stories. They kept alive a timeless and holy tradition—an ancient, cold-climate earth magic.

As the glaciers retreated and the climate became more temperate, new gods and new ways of worship spread into Europe with the first farmers and their descendents. Mother-goddesses, fertility cults, gods of the battlefield, and, eventually, Christianity took hold of the hearts and minds of the people. But, far to the north, the ancient shamanic spiritual traditions of the Ice Age lived on among the hunters and reindeer herders of the subarctic—the Lapps of northern Scandinavia and the people of Siberia—with deep spiritual connections across subarctic North America as well.

The shamanic tradition, with its roots deep in the Ice Age, survived into (almost) modern times among the hunters and herders of the far north. In the nineteenth and twentieth centuries, explorers, missionaries, and anthropologists observed and recorded some of these ancient earth-magic traditions among the Lapps and related peoples in Siberia and across North America and Greenland, in an almost continuous high-latitude swath of the planet. There is a strong element of continuity in this tradition across the northern world. Here, we find some of our most primitive "proto-Santa Claus" figures with roots that go deep into the past.

In this wintry northern world with its reindeer herds and chimney-and-hearth, we get our first glimpse of a recognizable Santa Claus figure. The shaman was capable of entering a trance state, sometimes aided by the consumption of a concoction of hallucinogenic plants; particularly popular was the fly agaric mushroom, which is, perhaps not coincidentally, the same contrasting red and white color of Santa Claus's suit! Dressed in a fur parka, the traditional subarctic shaman—a tribal elder, grey-bearded and well-fed—rose in spirit form through the hut's primitive chimney to fly through the air with the spirits of the herd, the reindeer. He returned with blessings—with gifts—for the people of the tribe.

Somehow, this primeval pre-Christian "Santa" is remembered and honored in the deep DNA of our modern Santa Claus, an almost unconscious memory of a very ancient cold-climate religious tradition. Figures very much like the "shamanic Santa" still—amazingly—survive in remote corners of Europe. And they contributed to the Santa Claus mythology we have carried with us into the twenty-first century.

2
The Real Saint Nick

ETERNAL GOD,
in your great love
you gave your servant Nicholas
a perpetual name for deeds of kindness on land and sea.
Grant that your Church may never cease to work
for the happiness of children,
the safety of sailors,
the relief of the poor
and the help of those who are tossed
by tempests of doubt or grief;
through Jesus Christ our Lord,
who lives and reigns with you and the Holy Spirit,
one God, now and forever.
Collect for the Feast of Saint Nicholas
from the Anglican tradition

Many people may have at least a vague awareness that our modern Santa Claus has some close connection to a Christian saint by the name of Nicholas. Even in the twenty-first century, Santa is still familiarly known as "Saint Nick" (often preceded by the descriptive "jolly, old"). The name *Santa Claus* itself (from the Dutch "Sinterklaas") makes this connection pretty clear: "Santa" from the Latin *sanctus*, meaning holy, and *Claus*, a Germanic-language nickname for Nicholas.

Saint Nicholas was, in fact, a real person. He was born into a wealthy Christian family around the year 270 in what is now modern Turkey but was then a Greek-speaking province of the Roman Empire. His name, Nikolaos, translates from the Greek as "victory of the people."

A Short Biography of Saint Nicholas

The facts of his life are shrouded in antiquity and legend, but he was apparently a good and holy man renowned for his generosity and for his loving care of the people of Myra, a port city on the Mediterranean coast of Turkey, where he served as bishop. He was one of the many bishops called together by the Emperor Constantine in 325 for the first Council of Nicaea, where Nicholas was a strong supporter of the Orthodox Christian position against the Arian heresy (which stated that Jesus did not always exist but had been created by God the Father). At one point in the Council, he is said to have defended his position in a fistfight with a dissenting bishop, a disturbance for which he was briefly imprisoned. The council eventually crafted the Nicene Creed, still a basic statement of the Christian faith that's recited regularly by churchgoers around the world (with no thought of Saint Nicholas's contributions). At Nicholas's death, on December 6, 343, the people of Myra unofficially proclaimed him to be a saint. His mortal remains became an object of veneration for centuries.

Beyond these bare facts is a far more expansive and rich tradition of legend surrounding the life of Saint Nicholas. Apparently, he was a man so holy that even as a baby he observed the fast days of the Church by refusing his mother's breast! A number of the best-known tales of Saint Nicholas beautifully illustrate why he became one of the most revered and popular saints in the Christian world. And we can see, over a thousand years later, some of his legendary kindness reflected in our own modern Santa Claus.

Santa Claus: Saint, Shaman, Symbol

Santa and the Serial Killer

During a time of famine in Myra, little boys were disappearing from the city's streets. Bishop Nicholas wanted to get to the bottom of this.

A heavenly guide led him to the cellars of an evil butcher, where he discovered a vat of little boys who had literally been pickled in brine. He brought the boys to life, saw that they were returned to their grateful families uneaten, and personally eliminated the evil butcher.

Nicholas, not content to let the condition continue that had produced this atrocity, then brought about a miraculous end to the famine. Unmanned ships loaded with grain arrived mysteriously at Myra's port. And Nicholas became a great hero of children and of the hungry poor.

Santa and the Sailors

Myra was a thriving port city in the fourth century, with ships coming and going, but famine was nevertheless common. In the thirteenth century, Jacobus de Voragine described this incident from the life of Nicholas:

> It was so on a time that all the province of Saint Nicholas suffered great famine, in such wise that victual failed. And then this holy man heard say that certain ships laden with wheat were arrived in the

haven. And anon he went thither and prayed the mariners that they would succour the perished at least with an hundred muyes of wheat of every ship. And they said: Father we dare not, for it is meted and measured, and we must give reckoning thereof in the garners of the Emperor in Alexandria. And the holy man said to them: Do this that I have said to you, and I promise, in the truth of God, that it shall not be lessed or minished when ye shall come to the garners. And when they had delivered so much out of every ship, they came into Alexandria and delivered the measure that they had received. And then they recounted the miracle to the ministers of the Emperor, and worshipped and praised strongly God and his servant Nicholas. Then this holy man distributed the wheat to every man after that he had need, in such wise that it sufficed for two years, not only for to sell, but also to sow.

Nicholas was a great friend of sailors. Once, when some local men were caught in a vicious storm at sea, they prayed to God for their lives—and their beloved Bishop Nicholas miraculously appeared at the helm of the ship and guided it safely home.

Through his intercession, Nicholas was able to protect the people of his city from attacks by pirates and from storms. He also restored cargo that had been lost at sea. As the patron saint of sailors, Nicholas's fame would spread throughout the Christian world.

Santa Fills His First Shoes

A poor man of Myra was facing the coming-of-age of his three daughters. Without dowries, the girls would be unable to find husbands, and their father feared that selling them into slavery and prostitution was their only alternative to starvation.

When Nicholas heard of their plight, he did more than merely pray for the girls; he took matters into his own hands. Under cover of night, he went to the man's home while the family slept. Then Nicholas threw three bags of gold, one for each girl's dowry, through an open window. The gold landed in their shoes, which had been drying beside the fireplace.

When the family awoke and found what was waiting for them by the fire, the father knew that only good Bishop Nicholas could have been behind such a generous and honor-saving gift. The bishop, however, said only that it was not he but God, who would always provide for the wants of the poor.

A Generous Saint

Nicholas's generosity to the poor and hungry became central to his legend. He was said to have spent all his own fortune in good works. He lived and died a simple servant of God and his people.

After his death, Nicholas's story spread throughout the Eastern Church. He continued to work miracles for those who called upon his help, and his tomb in the Cathedral of Myra became a place of prayer and pilgrimage.

Today, the anniversary of Nicholas's death, December 6, is still observed as his feast day. As we will see, the happy traditions of Saint Nicholas Day still enrich our lives, thanks in part to eleventh-century Crusaders who brought Saint Nicholas with them when they returned home to Europe.

And that's the next part of Santa Claus's story.

3

Saint Nicholas Comes to Europe

Nicholas, Saint of Children,
Loves to spend his wealth
On pretty toys for girls and boys,
Leaving them by stealth.
Nicholas, Saint of Sailors,
Children of the sea,
When their sails are torn by gales
Close at hand is he.
The wind in the rigging
Hears the sailors cry:
"Save us here, old Nicholas'
Save us there, good Nicholas!
Saint of Sailors,
Bring us safe
Home, high and dry!"
Eleanor Farjean

By the year 1000, Nicholas was a well-known and popular saint in the East, where he is still much revered in both the Russian and Greek Orthodox Churches as Nicholas the Wonderworker. But at the turn of the first millennium, his hometown of Myra was very much a part of the expanding and vigorous Islamic world, and his once-sacred bones lay almost forgotten in a disused cathedral in a thoroughly Muslim town.

In the year 1087, a group of sailors from the Italian port city of Bari took it upon themselves to reclaim (some say "steal") the holy bones of Saint Nicholas from what they called the "infidels" of Myra. They got away with most of the skeleton and various odds and ends from his tomb and brought them back to Bari. An anonymous Greek account describes what happened after the body of Saint Nicholas was transferred from Myra in Lycia to Bari in Italy:

> Now I should like to tell you, beloved, how the folk, running from the four corners of the city, gathered in Saint Nicholas's church, suffering from various

sicknesses. And there were cured that night and the following morning forty-seven men, women and children. And one of these was called Adralestus a man of noble and prominent family of the city of Bari, a victim of a terrible disease; and another was Armenius who was lame on his left side; and there were three epileptics, one deaf-mute, two with crippled arms, two lepers, three paralytics; there was also a certain Pisanus whose hands and feet were distorted. And many others were cured of whom I cannot give a detailed account. On the third day the people came in droves from all the environs to honor the sacred remains, as we have said. Among them seven men were cured up until the fourth watch of the day. And from the fourth watch till sunset fourteen others were cured. And on the fourth day twenty-nine others who were suffering dreadfully were cured. And not only those who suffered bodily ills obtained their health, but very many others who enjoyed bodily integrity, received conversion and salvation of soul, of whom I am unable to give a written account.

And on the fifth day our loyal patron Nicholas appeared in a vision to a certain monk whose name was Mark, of the monastery of Celius, bidding him to go to Bari and tell the people not to lose heart concerning the occurrence of miracles, "For by the will of God I am leaving the Roman world; but whither I go. I go on a visit, but here I shall dwell forever." But as another proof that they might know, the following event occurred. Before sunrise that day a man was cured who was tormented by an evil and deaf and dumb spirit! On the sixth day the Archbishop of Bari with four other Bishops of neighboring cities, together with their retinues of clergy and lay and a huge throng all came to reverence the saint, amid psalms and hymns and spiritual songs, justly honoring him who was honored and glorified by the Holy Trinity, and who in their last trials restores as citizens of heaven and equals of angels his servants and ministers.

Today, Saint Nicholas's relics still lie in the great Romanesque Cathedral of Saint Nicholas in Bari. Of course, Venice also claims a jumble of bones as the remains of Saint Nicholas, and bits and pieces of him are revered as relics in churches throughout the world. In the 1950s, however, physical anthropologists examined the almost-complete skeleton reputed to be the bones of Saint Nicholas in Bari. The anthropologists described the bones as being those of a robustly built man in his sixties who stood about five feet tall (a right jolly old elf?) and had a broken nose (from tussling at the Nicene Council?).

Santa and the Crusades

Over the next several centuries, tens of thousands of Western Europeans took part in a series of religious wars, known as the Crusades, against the Islamic rulers of the Middle East. Their ultimate goal was to conquer and make safe for Christian pilgrims the holy places associated with the life of Jesus Christ and his early followers. In fact, the Crusades, a series of wars motivated by religious faith at its most misguided, were a combination of prejudice and atrocity, faith and horror, with a mixed legacy we're still reaping today. Whatever else they did, however, the Crusades opened up trade routes—and the exchange of ideas—between the Muslim and Christian worlds. Returning Crusaders brought home with them a taste for exotic spices, a new knowledge of algebra and geography, and the legends (and relics) of dozens of formerly unknown Eastern saints.

The people of medieval Europe enthusiastically embraced a devotion to Saint Nicholas. His fame and popularity spread rapidly, and hundreds of churches were dedicated in his honor across the continent, from Ireland to Poland and Scandinavia to Sicily. Here was a kindly and approachable saint, interested in helping ordinary people who called upon him for aid and solace. As patron saint of children, sailors, and those in need, he appealed to millions of Christians. His lore and legend spread along the expanding sea routes of Europe wherever sailors traveled, and children everywhere grew up knowing they had a special heavenly friend who watched over and loved them. With a feast day early in the winter season and well within the orbit of Christmas, Saint Nicholas seemed to fit in perfectly with the generous and festive spirit of the Christmas season.

Santa and Christmas

In many ways, Christmas and Saint Nicholas evolved side-by-side. Like Christmas itself, the Christian Saint Nicholas became a rich and mysterious mixture of both Christian and pre-Christian images and rites. Over the centuries, the Christian saint took on aspects of old midwinter deities and semi-deities, solstice-time wild men who emerged from the dark forest ringing bells, bringing luck, and disciplining the children. He rode Odin's white horse over the rooftops, and he presided over feasting and imbibing of spirits in a sometimes very un-bishop-like way!

By the time of the Protestant Reformation, Saint Nicholas was well established in many parts of Europe as a wintertime giver of gifts to children, a symbol of both warmth and coziness and the darker challenges of the year's cold season.

We can trace the origins of our modern Santa Claus most directly to the Saint Nicholas Day customs and traditions of the Netherlands. Here, the character of the fourth-century bishop starts to become recognizably "Santa"—and it was the Dutch, with their devotion to the kind and generous saint, who helped turn the historical Saint Nicholas into the one we know and love today.

4
SINTERKLAAS KOMT! (SAINT NICHOLAS IS COMING!)

Saint Nicholas, good holy man!
Put on your cape as best you can,
Go, therewith, to Amsterdam,
From Amsterdam to Spain.
trans. from traditional Dutch children's song, 1810

A loud knock shakes the farmhouse door, and the children of the family scatter to the dark corners of the room. With great deference, Saint Nicholas—in the full regalia of a bishop of the Roman Catholic Church—is welcomed by Hans Myers, the master of the house. The bishop crouches as he enters the low doorway to accommodate his tall miter, blessing all who dwell therein. Before the door is closed against the chill December night, a dark and silent figure slips in, masked and dressed in furs and horned like a goat. Bishop Nicholas, who is in fact the priest of the parish, is offered a seat of honor by the fire. His mute companion, Belsnickel, stands by the fireplace with a horsewhip in one hand and an empty sack in the other.

Bishop Nicholas calls the children to his side. He seems to know everything about them. He asks them questions from the catechism, has them recite their prayers, and warns them of the dangers that await children who stray from the Church, who are lazy and disobedient, and who don't honor their elders. Belsnickel grunts and shakes his whip. The children know that bad boys and girls have been known to be carried off to hell in Belsnickel's sack, whipped all the way.

But Bishop Nicholas is satisfied, he tells Hans Myers. This is a good Christian home. There is hope for the children of this house. He stands to give a final blessing, and from under his robes he takes a handful of nuts and ginger cookies and throws them into the air. Saint Nicholas and Belsnickel move on to the next farmhouse, the children watching from the window to make sure Belsnickel is truly gone before they gather the goodies.

Nicholas the Gift Giver

By the time of the Protestant Reformation of the sixteenth and seventeenth centuries, Saint Nicholas was well established as the great December gift giver in a broad swath of Europe, from Holland and Belgium across the flat north of Germany and down into Austria and Central Europe. He was recognizable all across the continent: tall, dignified, and white-bearded, dressed in the traditional red vestments of a Roman Catholic bishop, complete with miter and crosier.

Through the bleak, dark days of early winter, children looked forward—with excitement and a certain amount of anxiety—to a visit from Saint Nicholas on the eve of his December sixth feast day. The established custom was for children to leave their shoes by the fireside or on the doorstep before they went to bed; sometimes, the shoes were filled with a treat for Saint Nicholas's horse. In the morning, good children would find their shoes filled with nuts and fruit and little gifts from the Saint. Badly behaved children may have been threatened that Saint Nicholas would leave them only a pile of ashes or a bundle of switches for future spankings, but then, as now, I suspect Santa's role as a disciplinarian was more bark than bite!

In some places, it was the Saint himself who visited homes on the evening of the fifth of December. A loud knock on the farmhouse door announced his arrival. Dressed as Bishop Nicholas, the parish priest or a village elder would be invited in with a respectful welcome. One or several mysterious companions in dark, raggedy clothes almost always accompanied him. These mysterious figures went by various names—Pelznickel, Belsnickel, and Aschenclaus (Ashy Nicholas), among others—usually variations of the Saint's own name. They were the kindly Saint's alter egos. While Saint Nicholas spoke gently to the children, his companion or companions stood mute in the firelight, often in demonic masks, holding whips and jingling bells. While Saint Nicholas might distribute candy and gifts from the bag he carried with him, his companions were there to remind children that bad behavior would have serious consequences. The sack full of toys and goodies we associate with Santa Claus was once as much of a threat as a delight for children. Bad kids could get taken away from home in that sack, to a place of eternal punishment!

Nowhere in old Europe was Saint Nicholas more revered than in Holland, as patron of both children and sailors in this country of traders and seafarers. Yet in few places was the Protestant Reformation more complete and radical than in the Netherlands. The power of Saint Nicholas's appeal and the celebrations associated with Saint Nicholas Day (Sinterklaas Dag) almost miraculously transcended this major shift in religious culture. In a country that had essentially abolished both Bishops and "saints," in the old Catholic sense, the traditional figure of kindly old Saint Nicholas remained virtually unchanged for centuries.

The Netherlands today is one of the most "post-Christian" and secular societies in the world. But Saint Nicholas still arrives by ship with great fanfare in dozens of Dutch cities and towns every November. Accompanied by his now somewhat-controversial and very politically incorrect servant Zwarte Piet (Black Pete), often dozens of Piets, he kicks off a holiday season that the Dutch love deeply. Just about every child in the Netherlands expects a visit from the "real" Saint Nicholas, and on the evening of December fifth, in the cold and drizzle that the Dutch call "Saint Nicholas weather," the streets are filled with family friends and favorite uncles dressed as Bishop Nicholas visiting homes with gifts and goodies. With that old knock at the door, Nicholas and Piet are welcomed into the warmth and comfort of the family home on a cold winter night. With a drink and a "cookie" (an old Dutch word), Saint Nicholas visits with the children, laughs and jokes with the grown-ups, and spreads good cheer. And the children of Holland go to bed confident that Saint Nicholas, riding his flying white horse from rooftop to rooftop, will be coming down the chimney that night to fill their shoes with gifts.

It was very much this Dutch Sinterklaas that was brought to New Amsterdam (modern-day New York) by colonists in the seventeenth century. Saint Nicholas came to America—and then New Amsterdam gave Santa Claus to the world.

5
SANTA CLAUS COMES TO AMERICA

Welcome, friend! St. Nicholas, welcome!
Bring no rod for us to-night!
While our voices bid thee welcome,
Every heart with joy is light

Tell us every fault and failing;
We will bear thy keenest railing
So we sing, so we sing:
Thou shalt tell us everything!

Fill each empty hand and basket;
'Tis thy little ones who ask it.
So we sing, so we sing:
Thou wilt bring us everything!
Mary Mapes Dodge, 1865

Picture yourself out and abroad on Long Island in the Colony of New York on a cold drizzly December night in 1713. A house looms ahead in the dense fog, and you make out solid oak beams and cedar shake shingles. This is the home of Gerrit and Geertje Ryder Snedecor, and its windows glow with warmth and light. Come closer now. Peek inside. . .

A group of neighbors have gathered: cousins, in-laws, friends, and numerous members of the Jamaica Reformed Dutch Church. They have all been born in America, and they are, at least nominally, loyal subjects of the King of England, but they retain a strong connection—in language and culture—with the "old Country," with Holland. Even now, in the eighteenth century, Long Island is a diverse community, and these farmers of Dutch heritage live in friendly cooperation with their "English" neighbors, Quakers, Presbyterians, Anglicans, and "free thinkers." During this time, western Long Island also has the highest percentage of African American slaves north of Virginia, and black people are an integral part of their community. But tonight, among themselves at home, the Snedecors and their friends and family are speaking Dutch. And watch! You'll see they have kept alive an ancient Netherlandish devotion to Sinterklaas, to Saint Nicholas—to Santa Claus.

In front of the roaring fire, the table is laden with good things to eat—crullers, cookies, oysters, roast turkeys, and smoked hams. Listen now! The children are being reminded that this is the night when Saint Nicholas will visit their homes, leaving toys and goodies in the shoes they have left by the fireside. The Dominie rises to give a blessing, and then Gerrit, with a pewter tankard of strong gin punch in his hand, offers a toast: "To Holland, to Sinterklaas, to our families, to us!"

Santa and Dutch Americans

In 1609, the Dutch East India Company ship, *Den Halve Maen* (Half Moon) entered one of the greatest natural harbors on the Earth, now known as New York Bay. Its English captain, Henry Hudson, sailed up the mighty river that now bears his name. He went as far as present-day Albany, claiming all the territory he explored for the Netherlands. In the decades that followed, the Dutch established the colony of New Netherlands, with its capital, New Amsterdam, at the foot of Manhattan Island.

The Protestant Dutch farmers and traders who settled New Netherlands—what is now northern New Jersey, the Hudson Valley, the City of New York, and western

Long Island—brought their love of the old Catholic Saint Nicholas with them. Sinterklaas rode his white horse over the rooftops of New Netherlands and came down the chimney to leave goodies and toys in well-behaved children's shoes on the eve of December 6, just as he had in Holland.

The Dutch colony peacefully changed hands in 1666 and was renamed New York by the British. But as British subjects, and, later, as citizens of the United States, families of Dutch descent preserved the traditions of Saint Nicholas Day. For generations, Sinterklaas continued to fill children's shoes—and later, stockings—at the firesides of the Van Burens, the DeGroats, the Snedecors (my mother's family), and their kin. But outside of these old New York Dutch families, Saint Nicholas was virtually unknown to most Americans until the publication of a truly remarkable poem in the 1820s.

The Night Before Christmas

Clement Clarke Moore (1779–1863) was born into a prominent New York City family, the son of the Episcopal Bishop of New York. A professor of Hebrew and Greek at Columbia College, and later at the Episcopal General Theological Seminary, which he helped establish, Clement Moore seems an unlikely "godfather" for the American Santa Claus. Moore's wife, Catherine, was a descendent of the Van Cortlandts, however, just the kind of family that would have still preserved the legend of Saint Nicholas in nineteenth-century New York.

And it was in Professor Moore's role as a family man, and not as a scholar, that he sat down and wrote "A Visit from Saint Nicholas" (now more popularly known as "'Twas the Night Before Christmas") on Christmas Eve 1822. He presented his whimsical poem as a Christmas gift to his wife and young children at a party for family and friends on Christmas Day, 1822. One of the party guests asked for a copy of the poem—and the rest, as the saying goes, is history!

In December of 1823, "A Visit from Saint Nicholas" was published anonymously in the *Troy Sentinel*. The poem went viral, at least by the standards of the early nineteenth century! Over the next several decades, it was reprinted literally thousands of times in newspapers and magazines throughout the English-speaking world. Professor Moore was somewhat reluctant to take credit for so "frivolous" a poem, but in 1844, it officially appeared in a collection of his more-scholarly works, under his own name.

We'll take a look at why Moore's "Saint Nick" became such a beloved figure, and how the legend and iconography of Santa Claus became so well established in American popular culture, in the next chapter. But first, I think the good professor's whimsical poem deserves a serious reading!

A Visit from St. Nicholas

'Twas the night before Christmas, when all through the house
Not a creature was stirring, not even a mouse;
The stockings were hung by the chimney with care,
In hopes that St. Nicholas soon would be there;
The children were nestled all snug in their beds,
While visions of sugar-plums danced in their heads;
And mamma in her 'kerchief, and I in my cap,
Had just settled our brains for a long winter's nap,
When out on the lawn there arose such a clatter,
I sprang from the bed to see what was the matter.
Away to the window I flew like a flash,
Tore open the shutters and threw up the sash.
The moon on the breast of the new-fallen snow
Gave the luster of mid-day to objects below,
When, what to my wondering eyes should appear,
But a miniature sleigh, and eight tiny reindeer,
With a little old driver, so lively and quick,
I knew in a moment it must be St. Nick.

Bill Palmer

More rapid than eagles his coursers they came,
And he whistled, and shouted, and called them by name;
"Now, Dasher! now, Dancer! now, Prancer and Vixen!
On, Comet! on, Cupid! on, Donder and Blitzen!
To the top of the porch! to the top of the wall!
Now dash away! dash away! dash away all!"
As dry leaves that before the wild hurricane fly,
When they meet with an obstacle, mount to the sky;
So up to the house-top the coursers they flew,
With the sleigh full of Toys, and St. Nicholas too.
And then, in a twinkling, I heard on the roof
The prancing and pawing of each little hoof.
As I drew in my head, and was turning around,
Down the chimney St. Nicholas came with a bound.
He was dressed all in fur, from his head to his foot,
And his clothes were all tarnished with ashes and soot;
A bundle of Toys he had flung on his back,
And he looked like a peddler just opening his pack.
His eyes—how they twinkled! his dimples how merry!
His cheeks were like roses, his nose like a cherry!
His droll little mouth was drawn up like a bow
And the beard of his chin was as white as the snow;
The stump of a pipe he held tight in his teeth,

Santa Claus: Saint, Shaman, Symbol

And the smoke it encircled his head like a wreath;
He had a broad face and a little round belly,
That shook when he laughed, like a bowlful of jelly.
He was chubby and plump, a right jolly old elf,
And I laughed when I saw him, in spite of myself;
A wink of his eye and a twist of his head,
Soon gave me to know I had nothing to dread;
He spoke not a word, but went straight to his work,
And filled all the stockings; then turned with a jerk,
And laying his finger aside of his nose,
And giving a nod, up the chimney he rose;
He sprang to his sleigh, to his team gave a whistle,
And away they all flew like the down of a thistle,
But I heard him exclaim, ere he drove out of sight,
"Happy Christmas to all, and to all a good-night."

Clement Clark Moore

6
Here Comes Santa Claus!

He comes—the brave old Christmas!
His sturdy steps I hear;
We will give him a hearty welcome,
As he comes again this a year!
English, 19th century

The Saint Nicholas that Clement Clarke Moore introduced to the world in his poem is a far cry from the Catholic bishop who was still (mysteriously) visiting Calvinist Holland—and a very long way, indeed, from the fourth-century wonder-working saint from Turkey. Moore's "right jolly old elf" who flew over the rooftops of old New York in a "miniature sleigh" pulled by "eight tiny reindeer" is a supernatural being with very little resemblance to a traditional Christian saint, although he is clearly identified as "Saint Nicholas," or simply "Saint Nick," several times in the poem. The father of the house, awakened by the clatter on the snowy lawn, recognized "in a moment" that the jolly, fur-clad little man with his snow-white beard, a "nose like a cherry," and a belly that "shook when he laughed like a bowlful of jelly" was Saint Nicholas, bringing gifts for the children.

A New Santa and a New Christmas

It's hard to say exactly where some of Moore's Saint Nicholas imagery comes from. Scholars of folklore believe that much of it is rooted in the various pre- or non-Christian beings that had long been attached to the Saint Nicholas figures of northern Europe. Moore was, after all, a scholar of ancient languages and lore. The poet's Saint Nicholas is obviously not a human holy man, but instead resembles a whole tribe of Germanic and Scandinavian trolls and their kin associated with mid-winter festivities, the family hearth, and earth magic. With the poem's magical flying reindeer (these seem to be completely Moore's own invention, though according to Lapp tradition, reindeer are, in fact, known to fly) and a laughter-prone little man who comes down the chimney, dressed all in fur, distributing gifts, Professor Moore of General Theological Seminary had wandered far afield from the traditional images of a Christian Christmas! (This may be why he was reluctant to admit to being the author of "A Visit from Saint Nicholas" for so many years.) Despite still calling him a saint, and transferring his visit from December 5 to Christmas Eve itself (which probably reflects changing customs in Dutch-American homes), Moore, a bishop's son and prominent Episcopal churchman, makes no reference at all to the birth of Jesus Christ or what is often referred to as the "real" meaning of Christmas.

And yet, although much transformed, Moore's Saint Nicholas was still very much the kindly December gift giver and friend to children he had been for centuries. Children's books, Sunday school publications, newspapers, and magazines spread and elaborated on the legend of the Dutch Sinterklaas (his name now Americanized as Santa Claus) to an enthusiastic American public. Along with the Christmas tree, first introduced to America by German immigrants at about the same time, Santa Claus was quickly becoming an essential part of mid-nineteenth-century Christmas celebrations.

Clement Moore's "right jolly old elf" was the version of Santa most often portrayed in the illustrations of the period: a fat, little gnome-like old man smoking a clay pipe and carrying a bag full of toys. The details of his costume varied considerably according to the imagination of the artist portraying him. Sometimes Santa Claus wore a fur-trimmed cloak with a hood, like many of old Europe's Saint Nicholas-related figures. He was dressed in green or brown as often as he was dressed in red. Sometimes he wore a little fur cap festooned with holly. Whatever the color of his clothes, Santa was always dressed for cold December weather—and he was definitely no longer clad in the vestments of a medieval Catholic bishop.

Santa and Thomas Nast

It was another New Yorker, the German-born illustrator Thomas Nast (1840–1902), who created the image of a Santa Claus that is almost—but not quite—our modern one.

Over the years, Nast drew Santa Claus literally hundreds of times, in settings as varied as lonely Civil War military encampments, children's Christmas parties, and in an ice-bound palace at the North Pole. Nast's Santa illustrations appeared on magazine covers, in newspapers, and in books.

Over the decades, Nast's portrayal of Santa Claus evolved from the tiny elf-like fellow to full human size. The immensely popular illustrations showed Santa on snow-covered roofs, driving a team of full-sized reindeer through the sky, and using a magic telescope to observe children's behavior, which he kept track of in a great, big book. Nast was incredibly influential in helping to create the Victorian Santa Claus that Americans came to know and love so well.

Santa and the United States of America

By the turn of the twentieth century, Santa Claus was as American as apple pie—and a symbol of the middle-class culture to which millions of immigrants aspired. Just about every American child knew then, as they still know, that Santa lives at the North Pole, wears a red, fur-trimmed suit, keeps track of who's naughty and nice, and flies through the air on a sleigh pulled by reindeer, delivering gifts to good boys and girls (who should be fast asleep) on Christmas

Eve. One of the most powerful myths of the modern world was becoming fully established.

The Santa Claus that our great-grandparents knew oversaw an increasingly child-centered and family-oriented Christmas. And the simple gifts he brought—an orange, a candy cane, a doll, a watercolor set—were still small enough to fit into a child's stocking. But that was about to change.

7
A "Saint" for the Twentieth Century

You better watch out!
You better not cry!
Better not pout,
I'm telling you why.
Santa Claus is coming to town!
John Frederick Coots and Haven Gillespie, 1930

More than 1500 years and several dozen human generations separate the Greek-speaking Turkish bishop Nicholas, and the Santa Claus who helped usher in the New Year in 1900. But the jolly old saint was still evolving.

Santa and Zeitgeist

As I've written about how the "real" Saint Nicholas evolved over time—and across three continents—into the ho-ho-hoing, milk-and-cookies-eating, sleigh-driving Santa Claus we have come to know as the great Christmas Eve gift giver, what has struck me, over and over again, is how closely the evolving "myth" of Santa Claus has expressed the *zeitgeist* ("the spirit of a culture") of his time and place.

We start with a wonder-working holy man, a high-ranking member of the established church, whose life was held up by that church as an example of service to Jesus Christ and the Christian community. This was the Nicholas of medieval Europe, a Christian saint called upon by the faithful for heavenly intercession in time of need, whose very bones were venerated as holy and miraculous.

The Saint Nicholas who survived the Reformation and brought gifts to the children of northern Europe on the eve of his December sixth feast day was still very much understood to be a Christian saint in the old tradition, but he had by then also taken on many of the attributes of the mysterious wintertime visitors and hearthside spirits of Germanic mythology. Victorian-era America took to Santa Claus in a big way. He was, it seems, the perfect personification of Christmas in a society that was becoming increasingly secular, while at the same time sentimentalizing childhood and "home sweet home." Santa represented a vision of cozy, middle-class comfort that was becoming accessible to more Americans—and was the aspiration of many more, including millions of new immigrants. For many of these new Americans, Santa Claus replaced the traditional Christmas-time gift givers of the "Old Country" (such as the Italian *La Befana* and the Slovak *Ježiško*).

Picture one of these immigrants, a Pennsylvania coal miner named Joe Smolenskas. Joe rises early on dark and cold December morning in 1913. His wife serves him a breakfast of ham and eggs and strong coffee in the gloomy kitchen while their four children still sleep. He kisses her goodbye at the door of the old frame house they rent from the Company, picks up the good lunch she has packed him, and then trudges through the shabby streets of Nanticoke.

Santa Claus: Saint, Shaman, Symbol

The dirty piles of snow on the side of the road are as high as his head as he heads toward the coal mine known as Evan's Colliery. But on this cold and dismal morning, Joe's step is jauntier than usual. At the end of the day, he knows he will collect his pay packet—and he'll have money to spend on Christmas. Thinking of the coming holiday, he can't help but smile.

There will be a feast at his brother-in-law's house on Christmas Eve—the traditional Holy Supper, with straw under the tablecloth in remembrance of the stable in Bethlehem and twelve meatless courses. Late that night, Joe will bring out the little presents he and his wife have bought for the children and put them under their Christmas tree. How excited they will be on Christmas morning!

Joe and his wife were born in the Old Country, in Lithuania, but his children are Americans, real Americans. In America, his children have taught him, Santa Claus comes to the homes of good children and brings them presents. Joe likes that idea. His children are good children, and he has worked hard and earned the money to give them the gifts that every good American child deserves. He will be their Santa Claus.

And on Christmas Day there will be no work in the mine. They will sing the happy Christmas hymns in the old language at Saint Joseph's Church. They will eat a big turkey dinner. His family will have a real American Christmas!

Santa and Materialism

Whether Santa Claus came down the chimney or through a tenement window, he was visiting more and more American homes as the twentieth century wore on. Except in the most prosperous families, the gifts Santa brought were still the kind of simple things that had always delighted children—an orange in the toe of a stocking, a bag of hard candy, a small doll, a story book, or a baseball glove. But Santa's gifts became more elaborate in the economic boom years of the 1920s, as incomes rose and cheaper mass-produced toys became available on the market.

My father was a great fan of Santa Claus. The Santa he learned to love in his 1920s childhood was already the familiar secular icon of the modern American Christmas. A jolly, fat man in a red, fur-trimmed suit? Check. A home at the North Pole? Check. A magical ability to observe who was being "naughty or nice"? Check. A sleigh pulled by flying reindeer? Check. A bringer of toys and goodies to good girls and boys on Christmas Eve? Check. Even his arrival at Macy's Department store in Herald Square on Thanksgiving Day (the first Macy's Thanksgiving Day Parade was in 1924, when my father was four years old) was already a part of the Santa Claus legend for a little boy growing up in New York City. The only thing missing from my father's Santa Claus legend was that beloved ninth reindeer, Rudolph. The story of the red-nosed outcast who saved a foggy Christmas was written by the advertising department of the Montgomery Ward department store and distributed by the millions in a giveaway booklet in the 1930s.

I presume that much of what my father learned about Santa Claus he learned sitting in his mother's lap—my beloved grandmother, who was born in New York City just twelve days before Christmas in 1895. (In fact, much of the iconography of Santa Claus was already well established in her turn-of-the-century childhood.) But while the Santa lore that had been passed on to my grandmother was from what might be called an "oral tradition" (supplemented by the many Christmas-themed children's publications and story books circulating at the time), my father's strongest connection to Santa Claus was through the airwaves of 1920s radio. When my father was a little boy, there was a broadcast message from Santa Claus on WOR radio on the nights leading up to Christmas, a source of great excitement to him. Hearing Santa's message, he could go happily to bed with visions of Christmas morning and a renewed motivation to be a good boy. My own love and admiration for Santa Claus is a gift from the man that little boy grew up to be.

The Depression and World War II may have pared down the expansion of Santa Claus's bounty, but the postwar era made up for it. Children of the Baby Boom of the 1950s and '60s were brought up with high expectations for Christmas morning. Santa was bringing shiny new bikes, talking dolls, battery-operated robots, and cowboy suits to good boys and girls. I was seven years old on Christmas Eve 1963, and even in my devoutly Catholic home, I went to bed dreaming of Santa Claus, not the Baby Jesus.

By the second half of the twentieth century, Santa Claus ruled over a Christmas that was bountiful (and materialistic) beyond the wildest dreams of our ancestors. His image had been enthusiastically taken up by the advertising industry to sell consumer goods—first children's toys, but later everything from electronic gadgets to luxury cars. Santa was literally *everywhere* in an expanding media culture.

His message, loud and clear (first in newspaper and magazine ads and later on radio, on TV, and online) was BUY, BUY, BUY. The department store—and later the mall—was now Santa's headquarters. And this all-about-the-presents Santa was becoming *the* icon of American consumer culture.

In the 1930s, '40s, and '50s, the Coca Cola Company produced dozens of advertisements, illustrated by Haddon Sundblom, which institutionalized the image of that jolly, white-bearded man in a red, fur-trimmed suit. Coca Cola exported the image around the globe, and today, this is the image that literally billions of earthlings recognize as THE Santa Claus. And in the dozens of brilliant illustrations that Sundblom created, Santa was always drinking that ultimate

American consumer beverage—Coke. The twentieth century Santa Claus was always trying to sell you something!

The Real Santa

But I propose that the spirit of Santa Claus—even in the most crassly commercial exploitation of his image—transcended the incredible excesses of twentieth-century materialism. A sizeable segment of the population still knew that Santa Claus didn't live at the mall, that he judged us not by how much money we had, but how "nice" (as opposed to "naughty") we were, and that his magic was about the simple joys of Christmas morning in your own living room, under your own Christmas tree. Children—and the people who love them—have always kept the *real* Santa Claus alive.

8

KEEP THE "SANTA" IN SANTA CLAUS!

O Saint of love,
be a guide for us
in our lives, we pray,
that we may
create joy for each other,
as you have done for so many.
from *St. Nikola an der Donau*, Austria

My mother is the unsung hero of the Christmases of my 1960s childhood. She did most of the holiday shopping and all the holiday cooking. I suspect she vacuumed up whole forests of shedding spruce needles over the years.

But in my family, Christmas really belonged to Dad. It started on Thanksgiving morning when Dad would call together what he called "his brood" from all corners of the house to make sure we saw the end of the Macy's Thanksgiving Day Parade and the arrival of Santa Claus. "That's the real Santa Claus, kids!" he'd tell us, his voice choked with emotion.

On the Sunday after Thanksgiving, my grandmother—my father's mother—would sit with each of us in turn for a serious review of the Gertz Department Store toy catalogue to pick out a special gift. We somehow understood that Grandma Palmer was able to communicate with Santa Claus, and that a department store in Jamaica, Queens, was one of his toy warehouses. And while, as I said, our mother did most of the Christmas work, it was Dad—we later learned—who personally made the bigger, and most "memorable" Christmas purchases: the really good telescope for me, the stingray bikes for Claire and Frank, and teenage Nancy's stereo record player, basketball tickets for Chucky.

We did Christmas Dad's way. The tree—the tallest white spruce available for ten dollars or less—was put up on Christmas Eve (not at the end of November as it is today—but it stayed up until January 6). The "tinsel" icicles had to be put on one strand at a time. The figure of the baby Jesus was placed in the manger scene before we went to bed on Christmas Eve after Midnight Mass. The next day we ate plum pudding.

Christmas in our home was not lavish. My parents sometimes struggled financially raising the five Palmer kids. But there was the smell of the Christmas tree, the hope of snow, a handful of Christmas cookies, and the absolute assurance that Santa was coming.

Santa was coming! Just ask Dad.

The Secular and the Sacred

My father's Christmas—the Christmas I learned to love in my parent's home and at my parish church—was a happy mix of holy mystery and earthly celebration. There were angels singing on the bubble lights on the tree and

Santa Claus: Saint, Shaman, Symbol

Santa's sleigh on the roof. The secular and the sacred aspects of the season seemed to perfectly complement each other in those simple Christmases of my childhood. They weren't in opposition with one another. I'm writing this on the eleventh day of the traditional twelve days of Christmas, which end with the Feast of the Epiphany on January sixth. For Christians, these twelve days are meant to be the heart of the holiday season—but those of us who try to keep Christmas going into early January are really at odds with the twenty-first century.

For most Americans, Christmas is long over. The holiday season that began when the mob stormed the gates of the mall very, very early on the morning after Thanksgiving ("Black Friday") ended on the day after Christmas, when disappointed crowds filled the stores to return gifts they didn't like and buy what they really wanted. That makes me sad. I'm still thinking about Santa Claus on this cold January morning!

This cultural conflict between the "secular" and the "sacred" celebration of Christmas is a very old one. The Church has been railing against the materialism of the holiday for over a thousand years. The debate over who "owns" Christmas has become particularly mean-spirited in recent years. Maybe it's time we reclaim Santa Claus as the one figure who might be able to bridge this gap and help us all—Christians, non-Christians, and secularists alike—celebrate a more meaningful and happier December holiday.

More and more people are becoming disillusioned with what I'll call the consumer-goods Christmas, the Christmas that's headquartered at the mall. Let's face it—all those gifts don't make us happy. With the economic realities of twenty-first-century America, we can't really afford them anyway. Since Santa's image has been used to sell us all this "stuff," many of us have understandably become a bit cynical about the jolly man in the red suit. Some religious people, completely forgetting Santa's saintly roots, have gone so far as to portray the good saint as the "anti-Baby Jesus." They see Santa Claus as presiding over a holiday of materialism and greed in direct competition with—and in opposition to—the real spirit and meaning of Christmas.

But Santa Claus, like Christmas itself, continues to offer us something that truly transcends our grown-up cynicism and disillusionment. To fully embrace Santa Claus is to also embrace the magic we knew through him as children. To understand him is to acknowledge his embodiment of the collective hopes and aspirations of generations of our ancestors who created in him a perfect symbol of both Christian virtue—a loving generosity toward all—and the old solstice celebration of life and joy in the darkest days of the year. Santa is a myth that gives us hope.

Santa Claus: Saint, Shaman, Symbol

The Santa Myth

John Ruskin wrote, "A myth, in its simplest definition, is a story with a meaning attached to it other than it seems to have at first." Myths are narratives that give deeper meaning to our lives. They reveal a reality that lies both within and beyond the world we see and touch. Much of our understanding of the world and of our place in it is rooted in the myths we choose, as individuals and as communities, to believe. Human beings have lived and died, have killed and been killed, in the name of these great mythic beliefs and the ideologies they support.

What can we, as mortal beings, really *know* to be absolutely true and unchanging in a universe that continues to reveal itself through time and space but remains, essentially, a great—and I believe, a holy—mystery? Religion, science, technology, politics, philosophy—the whole intellectual and spiritual superstructure we call human civilization—is built on an essentially fragile foundation of "faith," whether it be faith in a transcendent "spirituality," in the rationality of the "scientific method," or something more like the "me-first" materialism merging into nihilism that seems to be ruling the hearts and minds of so many of us in the modern Western world. They're all stories we tell ourselves to make sense of the world. They're myths.

I guess I have to admit that the myths I live by, like most everyone else's, are cobbled together from various sources and experiences. This is one of the gifts—and the challenges—of being a modern, thinking person: that our own personal beliefs can be informed by an ever-increasing knowledge base of world history, science, politics, and spiritual tradition from which we must choose our own tools to help us interpret and understand ourselves and our place in the world. As for me, I see myself as a "cafeteria-style" mystic, an Anglican Christian, an intellectual, a man of good taste, a family man, a sentimentalist. And I confess: I still believe in Santa.

To live an intentional, spiritual life, we have the responsibility to choose the myths that shape our life. Personally, I choose to believe in Santa Claus. He is wonderful and magical. He is a very special part of my memories of childhood Christmases long ago. And he remains, for me, a messenger of the true meaning of Christmas.

I can't prove his existence, of course. I can't rationalize it. But untold generations have placed their faith and their hopes for a Merry Christmas, a Happy New Year, and a better world in Santa Claus—and so do I. He personifies a generous and jolly heart, a tender love of children, a deep desire to help the poor, and the holy mysteries of the cold and wintry Earth. He symbolizes the simple pleasures of home and family life and childhood—the smell of the Christmas tree, the crunch of a sugar cookie, the folks around the table. He urges us to be our best selves, with the promise of enjoying the bounty of Creation in a happy holiday that sets our sights on the possibilities of a more peaceful, generous, and happy world. And while not all, and not everyone's, Christmas memories are happy and "magical," I believe Santa Claus's spirit has nevertheless been with us, in all of his many guises—as shaman, as saint, and as symbol—as far back as any of us can know.

While much of the world may seem to have forgotten his roots as Winter Solstice holy man and Christian saint, Santa Claus remains a powerful symbol for good in the world, an inspiration to the kind-hearted and the generous. *Santa* is the Latin word for "holy"—and I for one believe we need to put the "Santa" back in Santa Claus.

And so I'd like to propose this as a slogan, right along with the old (and more exclusionary) "Keep Christ in Christmas"—

Let's keep the "Santa" in Santa Claus!

At the Back of the North Wind
Author: George MacDonald
(edited and updated
by Sheila Stewart)
Price: US $19.95
Paperback
Ebook Available
312 pages
ISBN: 978-1-933630-84-7

George MacDonald's fantasies inspired C.S. Lewis, author of the Narnia Chronicles. Now Anamchara Books brings today's readers a modern-language version of MacDonald's classic story. Diamond, a child of Victorian London, sleeps above the stable. When he hears a voice talking to him through a crack in the wall, a new world of mystery and meaning opens up to him. North Wind, the beautiful woman who can be either tiny or immense, sweeps him up in her arms and carries him over the city's dark streets. Their adventures together reveal the glimmer of love and wonder shining even within the grim reality of poverty and despair.

"One of George MacDonald's most engaging fantasies is here attractively rendered in an up-to-date style, faithfully conveying its mythic impact."
—**Rolland Hein**, author of *The Harmony Within: The Spiritual Vision of George MacDonald* and *George MacDonald: Victorian Mythmaker.*

Water from an Ancient Well: Celtic Spirituality for Modern Life
Author: Kenneth McIntosh
Price: $24.95
Paperback
Ebook Available
352 pages
ISBN: 978-1-933630-98-4

Discover the world of the ancient Celtic Christians and find practical insights for living in the twenty-first century. Using storytelling, careful research, and personal experience, the author invites you to get to know Brendan and Brigid, Columba and Patrick, as well as Myrddin (better known as Merlin) and other lesser-known figures from the great pageant of Celtic history. These stories both entertain and inspire; rooted in legend and history, they offer us here-and-now hope and insight.

"When I was reading *Water from an Ancient Well*, I sometimes felt like I taking a spiritual pilgrimage to Cano Cristales, the most beautiful river in the world or the river of five colors. Located near the town of La Macarena in Colombia, South America, the river is famous for its colorful blotches of blue, green, black, and red causing some to call it the river that ran away to paradise. If you want to run away to paradise for a couple of days, and drink living water from a source unlike any other, read Kenneth McIntosh's deeply satisfying book."
—***Leonard Sweet***, best-selling author and professor.

Earth Afire with God: Celtic Prayers for Ordinary Life
Author: Anamchara Books
Price: $12.95
Paperback
Ebook Available
120 pages
ISBN: 978-1-933630-96-0

Here are prayers and blessings to sanctify your daily life. They will remind you to look for the holiness of the everyday; they will show you the real presence of God in Creation. Illumine your life with the ancient Celts' perspective on prayer. Each glimpse we have of the Earth's beauty, each ordinary sound we hear, every bite of food we eat, and even our daily routines, can all reveal God.

Kenneth McIntosh, author of *Water from an Ancient Well, Celtic Spirituality for Modern Life*, writes, "The folks at Anamchara Books have done a real favor for all of us who struggle to integrate communion with God into our increasingly busy and complex lives. These short but powerful prayers connect daily routines—washing in the morning, starting the car, seeing a child off to school, or sitting at our computer—with the comforting Divine Presence. This book knocks the dust off ancient treasures—such as selections from the Carmina Gadelica—and also introduces some lovely new prayers, all written from the Celtic perspective."

Anamchara Books
Books to Inspire
Your Spiritual Journey

In Celtic Christianity, an *anamchara* is a soul friend, a companion and mentor (often across the miles and the years) on the spiritual journey. Soul friendship entails a commitment to both accept and challenge, to reach across all divisions in a search for the wisdom and truth at the heart of our lives.

At Anamchara Books, we are committed to creating a community of soul friends by publishing books that lead us into deeper relationships with God, the Earth, and each other. These books connect us with the great mystics of the past, as well as with more modern spiritual thinkers. They are designed to build bridges, shaping an inclusive spirituality where we all can grow.

To find out more about Anamchara Books and order our books, visit **www.AnamcharaBooks.com** today.

Anamchara Books
Vestal, New York 13850
www.AnamcharaBooks.com